A

CHRISTMAS

TO

REMEMBER

Charlie Jones

SEVEN LOCKS PRESS

Santa Ana, California

Seven Locks Press
P.O. Box 25689
Santa Ana, CA 92799
(800) 354-5348

Individual Sales. This book is available through most bookstores or can be ordered directly from Seven Locks Press at the address above.

Quantity Sales. Special discounts are available on quantity purchases by corporations, associations, and others. For details, contact the "Special Sales Department" at the publisher's address above.

Printed in the United States of America

Library of Congress Cataloging-in-Publication Data
is available from the publisher
ISBN 1-931643-56-3

Cover and Interior Design by Heather Buchman

Dedicated to all the moms and dads (and grandmothers and grandfathers . . .) who make Christmas such a special time of the year. And to the memory of my friend, Pat Hart, who gave so much to the men and women who fought in Vietnam.

A CHRISTMAS TO REMEMBER takes us back to those wonderful days when we were young and for the most part, still believed in Santa Claus. At least we didn't want to take any chances and miss out on his trip down the chimney.

A CHRISTMAS TO REMEMBER is a present of special Christmas memories from my friends to you. It reminds us that it was "just yesterday" when it was so hard to go to sleep on Christmas Eve, and all the time we had to wait after opening our presents on Christmas morning until next year's Christmas. It seemed like a lifetime.

A CHRISTMAS TO REMEMBER may be more than a "long ago." *A Christmas to Remember* can happen at any time, at any place, at any age.

— *Charlie Jones*

COMMENTS FROM
THE REINDEER'S BARN

"Did you know that reindeer have small glands between their rear toes which leave a trail of scent so that the rest of them can follow Rudolph, even in a thick fog."

— *Santa*

"I remember the time there was no snow and Santa made us wear roller skates."

— *Dasher*

"What about the Christmas Eve Santa slept late and we had to skip every other rooftop?"

— *Dancer*

"Remember when the marine layer was so bad we missed Escondido and had to go *back*?!"

— *Prancer*

"How about the time during the "Cold War" when the Russians gave us a MIG jet escort over Moscow."

— *Vixen*

"Each year we try to surprise a part of the world that doesn't believe in us yet. It always works."

— *Comet*

"I remember that rooftop in London when Santa surprised a chimney sweep. I thought they both would have a heart attack."

— *Cupid*

"What about when we re-crossed the International Dateline and lost track of time. Some kids got their presents a day early and other kids got theirs a day late!"

— *Donner*

"Remember when we were chasing Air Force One on Christmas Eve and we had to keep dodging heat-seeking missiles until they *finally* believed it was *really* us?"

— *Blitzen*

"Hey, what am I doing down here as the last of the reindeers? I deserve top billing. IMMEDIATELY ... or I'll turn my nose off. Then you'll be sorry ...."

— *Rudolph*

M E R R Y   C H R I S T M A S

A

CHRISTMAS

TO

REMEMBER

— One —

Surprising Santa Claus

I grew up in Glenview, Illinois, just north of Chicago. Our family had a Christmas Eve tradition in which Mom would pile all seven kids in the family station wagon and drive us around to see the houses decorated in Christmas lights to get us into the proper spirit.

The Christmas Eve I most remember was when I was nine years old. When we got back, we clamored out of the station wagon and rushed into the house. We discovered Dad in his favorite chair in the living room, and he was all tied up.

"What happened?" we shouted.

Dad explained that he was upstairs when he heard a noise. So naturally, he came down to investigate, and he surprised Santa Claus.

Well, Santa Claus tied him up, ate the cookies, drank the milk, took the carrots for the reindeer, stuffed the stockings, left the presents under the tree, and then he put his finger to the side of his nose and went back up the chimney.

Dad cautioned us to be *very* careful, and *not* surprise Santa Claus or he would tie us up, too.

— *Felicia*

Two

MY RED WAGON

I was seven years old and we lived on a farm. More than anything I wanted a red wagon for Christmas. My prospects weren't all that good because we were very poor. Still every night I always remembered Santa Claus in my prayers, and I always mentioned the red wagon.

When I awoke on Christmas morning, I didn't know whether or not to get my hopes up. But there it was right next to the tree, my very own red wagon. I thought it was the best red wagon in the whole world, even though it looked little strange because it was somewhat fat in the middle.

When I grew older, I learned the story of my red wagon. My parents didn't have enough money to buy me a red wagon, so my father got an old wheelbarrow and removed the handles. He then scavenged wheels from a pushcart, welded it together, put on a handle, and painted it all red.

It was then I realized the real Santa Claus was my father, and in fact I really did have the best red wagon in the whole world.

— *Dempsey*

Three

THE OTHER SIDE OF THE TRACKS

As a kid in Muskogee, Oklahoma, we never had much of a Christmas. There were six of us, including Momma. Our dad had left long ago. Momma tried to hold down two jobs, but the cleaning one took so much out of her that she had to stop delivering newspapers until I was old enough to take on that responsibility myself.

There was a Baptist Church in town that looked after us, especially during the holidays. Every Christmas Eve until the year I left to join the Marines, they would come by with food, clothing, and gifts. The presents were always wrapped in colorful paper with great big bows.

I never told anyone because I was too ashamed, but those were the only Christmas presents I ever had until I was a grown man.

Now I wish I could go back to Muskogee, and on a Sunday morning in my Marine dress uniform, walk down to the front of that church and tell those same people how much their kindness meant to me as a kid.

Instead, I try to do the next best thing. Every Christmas Eve, my wife and I, along with our three boys, gather up food, clothes, and lots of presents all with great big bows. We take them to the families who live just like I did, on the other side of the tracks.

— *Kareem*

Four

THE GRINCH AT CHRISTMAS

Each Christmas, we are delighted with San Diego's Old Globe production of the Dr. Seuss classic, *How The Grinch Stole Christmas*. This spectacular presentation is our family's secret ingredient to instantly put us in the Christmas spirit.

With our busy lives, careers, and our kids running everywhere, it is almost too easy to continue life as normal and not slow down enough to even realize that the holiday season is upon us. But, as the lights darken in the theater and we experience the Grinch learning the essence of the season through the eyes of Cindy Loo Who, our hearts are warmed and we are splendidly overwhelmed with the Christmas spirit.

As we leave the theater, suddenly it *is* Christmas, and the feeling is as good as Christmas morning itself. We try to remember the words and the message of the Grinch throughout the year:

Then the Grinch thought of something he hadn't before! "Maybe Christmas," he thought, "doesn't come from a store. Maybe Christmas . . . perhaps . . . means a little bit more!"

It isn't about the number of presents but rather the amount of love you carry in your heart and give others all year long that matters most.

— *Greg & Kim*

Five

UP ON THE HOUSETOP

One Christmas Eve, my former husband had celebrated a little too much at a party (so we won't use his name or mine). In truth, he was drunk. *Really* drunk.

When we arrived home about midnight, he got out of the car, took the ladder out of the garage, and leaned it up against the house. Then he went inside, unlocked the cabinet, took out his shotgun, filled his pockets with shells, and went back outside . . . with the gun.

Disregarding all my pleas as I trailed along behind him, he climbed up the ladder onto the roof of the house and fired his shotgun into the air. As you can well imagine, you could hear the explosion blocks way. So it was only moments before our neighbors came streaming out of their homes to find out what was going on.

When it became apparent *where* the explosion had come from, they gathered in our front yard and started yelling, "*What* are you *doing*?"

My former husband shouted back, "I'm sick to death of those reindeer, *especially* the one with the blinking red nose. He thinks he's an airplane when he flies overhead! If those reindeer try to land on my roof tonight, I'm going to shoot every one of them!"

— *Anonymous*

— *Six* —

THE GOLD SANDALS

Our entire family—all twenty-three of us—get together both Christmas Eve and Christmas Day every year. When I was twenty-four, I was dating this nice guy, Bob. So naturally, he was invited to spend Christmas with us and participate in our gift exchange.

As Christmas drew near, Bob told me he wanted to give me my gift in front of the whole family on Christmas Eve. He kept dropping hints, which left the impression it might be an engagement ring. He said my dad knew what it was and that we should really have a video recorder there to capture the opening of his gift. He wanted us to have the tape for our future.

The last thing I wanted was an engagement ring! Bob was truly a great guy, but I wasn't thinking about marriage with anyone at that particular time in my life.

Gift exchange time came at last. All of us gathered around and the video recorder was set up. When it was my turn to open Bob's gift, excitement took over. The video recorder was turned on, cameras were ready, and everyone was on the edge of their seats.

I was about to pass out. I just wanted to crawl under the couch and disappear. At one point, I pinched myself to see if it was just a bad dream. I actually pinched myself so hard that I still have the scar.

Bob had warned me previously not to be fooled by the size of the box. My hands were shaking, but I persevered in getting it unwrapped. When I finally opened the top of the box, I couldn't believe my eyes. I let out a shrieking holler, threw my arms in the air in a victorious fashion, and yelled "YES!"

The box contained a pair of hideous clunky gold sandals that is our family tradition to pass around to unsuspecting members. Of course, they were all in on the joke.

Everyone thought I would be so excited to think it was an engagement ring, and then let down when I realized it was the clunky gold sandals. Nobody expected me to be so relieved.

Needless to say, Bob was none too thrilled about my joy at receiving that hideous pair of sandals, and he and I are no longer dating. But one thing for sure, *every* Christmas "The Gold Sandals" story gets told.

— *Tina*

— *Seven* —

THE SPECIAL MEANING
OF CHRISTMAS

It was Easter 1996, when we flew to Kalliningrad, Russia, to adopt a little boy my wife Mary and I had identified by video seven months earlier. After three miscarriages, a stillborn baby girl, and two failed local adoptions, we had been through a lot. We knew we wanted more children than our one little girl, and after a lot of prayer and discussion, we felt led to go to Russia.

Mary's sister and husband had traveled there a year earlier and brought home a precious little girl. They had spoken of the children it had been difficult for them to leave behind, the children in orphanages who had little hope of ever getting out. They had returned committed to trying to do something and, with all their new contacts, set about making it possible for American couples to adopt in Russia. It was their videos that helped convince us we should pursue a Russian adoption.

We had no idea that our desire to bring back a child would lead to two, "brothers" according to the Russian authorities, but as different looking as night and day. Still, they were now brothers in our family, and we set about teaching them about America. The oldest, Erik, was five and the youngest, Timmy, was two and a half. Both spoke only Russian.

We live in southern California where it is a whole lot warmer than they were used to, and where every day in their new home was like a day in Disneyland. The boys had never had their own room, watched TV, been able to eat as much as they wanted, or go places in a car. It was sensory overload, and they loved it.

When Christmas rolled around eight months later, they had no idea why their cousins were suddenly getting so excited and kept talking about Santa Claus. They had never heard about the jolly old man with the long white beard, all dressed in red, and couldn't believe he would come down chimneys to deliver toys to children! This was better than Disneyland!!

When Christmas Eve finally arrived, we were very excited to introduce them to the traditions Mary and I had grown up with. We both had wonderful memories of Christmas and couldn't wait to establish them in our new family.

We began by going to church, and then returned home to set out milk, cookies, and carrots by the fireplace for Santa and his reindeer. After tucking the kids into bed, we read *The Christmas Story* and *Twas The Night Before Christmas*. As they snuggled in their beds, we reminded them that if they listened very closely they might hear Santa and his reindeer up on the roof.

While they were saying prayers with Mary, I carefully slipped outside and began throwing pebbles up on the roof and shaking little bells. I even threw in a few "Ho Ho Ho's" to complete the ruse. When I snuck back in, I found the boys wide awake with their eyes big as saucers and each wanting to tell me all about what they had just heard.

It was the beginning of a very special Christmas for all of us, and one that Mary and I will never forget. It was magical to bring such joy to Erik and Timmy, and humbling to see how the Lord had worked out such a special gift for us. It reminded us that the root of joy is gratefulness. We hope one day that our boys will be able to appreciate all that the Lord has done for them and be able to pass on to their kids our traditions and the special meaning of Christmas.

— Rolf

Eight

ADOPT A FAMILY

We are a large family—seven kids: two boys, five girls. We were beginning to notice gifts for the adults were becoming a bit troublesome and almost like work.

I am not sure what happened first. We lost my little brother, the youngest child in our family, to a heart condition. In his honor we "adopted" a family for Christmas, and money that would have been spent on unnecessary gifts for each other was used to share "his love."

Our tradition continues, and this year my parents and I gave to a single mom with four children. It's amazing how love and giving circles around if people keep the focus on what it's truly about. This mother went home and told her children, and the eldest said, "I can't wait 'til we're able to do this for someone else, because now I know how much it means."

Love, gifts, giving, Christmas . . . it all started with the greatest and most selfless gift of all—an innocent infant sent by His Father for us. God Bless.

— *Patti*

— *Nine* —

THE BLUE LAMB

My young daughter, about seven years old, and my dad were browsing in an antique store while my husband and I did our final Christmas Eve shopping.

Sydney, my daughter, had taken all the change from her piggy bank and was carrying it around in her pockets. In the antique store, she walked right up to the saleswoman, dumped her change on the counter, told the woman she needed a Christmas present for her mother, and asked if the store had anything for that much money.

My dad stood there, sort of horrified. Then the saleswoman said, "I think I have just the thing."

In the display window was a decorated Christmas tree. The woman took a small, blue, stuffed lamb ornament off the tree and asked Sydney if she thought her mother would like it.

The saleswoman carefully put the lamb in a gift box and wrapped it in Christmas paper. My dad choked back a couple of tears when he and Sydney left the store.

When I opened the present the next day, I thought it was very sweet. Then, while Sydney was distracted opening her presents, my dad told us the real story of the blue lamb. We all cried a little.

I will always be grateful for the spirit of Christmas that the saleswoman shared with my daughter. And my family will always remember "The Christmas of the Blue Lamb."

— *Susan*

Ten

"HE CAME!"

I was about five or six years of age and, of course, thoroughly believed in Santa Claus. My family lived in Cleveland, Ohio, at the time. It was cold, with snow forecast.

Like any child in that era, I wanted Christmas morning to arrive as soon as possible. To speed this up, I was in bed at about 6:30 P.M. on Christmas Eve. After tossing and turning for what seemed like hours in anticipation of the coming morning, I finally fell asleep.

Upon awakening at about 4:30 A.M. in the morning, I looked out my small, second story bedroom window. The snow must have been two feet deep, completely covering everything within my view. The only phenomena to mar the otherwise perfect snowfall were the tracks in our small backyard—tracks that started in the *middle* of the lot and *ended* at my house. I thought, *Could these be Santa's reindeer?*

Leaving my nose and breath imprint on the window, I slipped very quietly past my parents' bedroom to the small staircase leading down into our living room. About halfway down, I could smell the pine scent of the beautifully decorated tree. Then, all of a sudden, there it was. The tree was completely lit up.

Looking to the end table where I had left milk and cookies for Santa, I could see that several of the cookies were half eaten and the milk was almost completely gone. As my eyes darted back to the tree, I saw a small electric train going on a strange course between some wrapped gifts. And a fort, complete with cowboys and soldiers inside, and Indians attacking on the outside. Santa had even made it look like a battle was going on. Then I turned to my left, and there on a chair was a ball and glove, and below was a brand new red football helmet.

I leaned back from between the dividers in the banister and whispered, "He Came!"

— *Angelo*

Eleven

A CHRISTMAS LESSON

Christmases on our Iowa farm were always good. Mom had a real knack for decorating a tree, and ours always seemed special to me. But 1949 was a tough year for farmers, and we never seemed to have money for anything other than food or clothes. In the past, Santa Claus and Christmas morning always brought something special for us kids, regardless of the lack of bountiful crops or low cattle prices. So, as usual, our hope for this Christmas was very high.

Our house on the hill had no inside plumbing or running water. In the kitchen was a small hand pump called a pitcher pump, right next to the sink. For hot water, Mom had to heat it on the cookstove, or sometimes she would use the heat stove in the living room. That also meant the only bathroom facility was an outhouse about fifty feet from the house on the hill.

We may not have had inside plumbing, but thanks to something called the REA (Rural Electric Association) that was formed after World War II, we did have electricity in our house. The most important thing it provided was lights, and the second most important thing was power for a radio. We spent hours every evening listening to the radio, which even had a phonograph so we could play Christmas records during the season.

On Christmas morning, the drill was for us kids to line up according to age at the top of the stairs going down into the living room. I was the third oldest, so my two sisters would be in front of me and my little brother would be last behind me.

On Christmas morning of 1949, we awoke early, around 6:00 A.M. It was bitter cold in our bedrooms, but we didn't care. All we could think of was going down those stairs and seeing what Santa had left each of us. Mom and Dad were not real happy about the early hour, but they told us to line up and they would go down, turn up the heat, and light the tree.

Standing in line and waiting seemed to be forever for me, so I devised a plan. I yelled down the stairs to Mom, "I have to go to the bathroom real bad, Mom!" That, of course, would require I go down the stairs and out the door into the winter, run the fifty feet to the outhouse, relieve myself, then return somehow without freezing, and go upstairs and get back in line.

This also meant that I would be going through the living room past the Christmas tree and all those toys, and just maybe I could sneak in a preview peek before anyone else! Mom's reply was "Okay, but don't you look at the Christmas tree. You just make a beeline for the door and the outhouse!"

I leaped down the stairs two at a time, ran out the door without looking, and headed to the outhouse. It was freezing cold and once inside the small structure, there was no way I could go to the bathroom. It was too cold and all I could think of was that Christmas tree. I waited the appropriate length of time and then headed back to the house, running as fast as my eight-year-old legs would carry me to prevent freezing and to try and see Santa's toys.

When I entered the house, I headed for the stairs to go up and get back in line, but I noticed that Mom and Dad were now in the kitchen and had their backs to me. Here was my chance! Right before I hit that first step heading up, I took a quick peek at the tree and lo' and behold, under it was the neatest electric train I had ever seen! By some quick deduction, I knew that it had to be mine. My sisters didn't like trains and my brother was much too young for an electric train. I just knew it was mine and this was going to be the best Christmas ever!

I took the steps two at a time going up and quickly got back in line. I was bursting with excitement, so much so that I turned to my younger brother and whispered, "I got an electric train from Santa; I saw it, and it is the best train in the whole world!"

My brother didn't say a thing, but I had whispered just a little too loud and my oldest sister heard me and yelled down to Mom, "Ken peeked and saw his Santa gift. That's not fair. We are supposed to go down and see the gifts all at the same time!"

I was caught and now all I heard was Dad coming up those stairs, and suddenly there he was towering over me. "Did you look at that tree when you went down to the bathroom?" he bellowed.

"No, Dad, I didn't see a thing," I meekly replied.

My sister countered, "He just told his brother Santa left him a train. How would he know if he hadn't peeked?" I was in big trouble, and all I could think of was that beautiful train downstairs under the tree, and that I might not get to play with it before it went back to Santa.

Mom and Dad conferred and my sentence was finally announced. The others were going to be allowed to go down and get their Santa gifts and I was going to have to stay upstairs until they decided I had been punished enough.

It is now fifty-five years later and I cannot remember exactly how long I had to wait; but at the time, it seemed like an eternity. Maybe it was five minutes or fifteen, I am not sure, but to stand up there and hear my sisters and brother having the time of their lives with their new toys was torture even for one minute. Finally, I was allowed to join them.

That morning I learned a big lesson about doing as I was told. I still have that train packed away in a box in our storage room in this big modern house (with indoor plumbing) in which my wife and I now live. The box is covered with dust, and the last time I took it out, about six or so years ago, I couldn't even get the train to run. However, it still reminds me of the time I tried to sneak a peek when I was told not to.

Both Mom and Dad have been gone now for many years, but they taught me a very big lesson that Christmas morning of 1949. And I love them for it.

— Ken Fouts, Jr.

Twelve

A MAGIC BUTTON

I'm eleven years old now, but I remember it snowing a few weeks before Christmas when I was in the fourth grade and living in Raleigh, North Carolina. My neighborhood friends and I played almost all day, having snowball fights and then video games inside when we got cold.

That's when my grandparents came from Kansas. They brought both their dogs, Shadow and Noel, to play with my dog, Boomer, so as not to have them feel left out.

I was counting off the days to Christmas when Christmas Eve finally arrived. I think that is my least favorite day of the year because you have so much anticipation for the following day. That night, Dad went on the Internet to a Web site that tracks where Santa is on the globe. When I went to bed, Santa was in Europe.

Christmas Day arrived, and I would not sneak downstairs to look before my parents (like I did last year) because it ruins the surprise. How was it? Well, I say this every Christmas night: "I wish I had a magic button that I could push to repeat this day."

— *Parker*

Thirteen

CHRISTMAS TREE LANE

Every Christmas Eve, our family climbs in the car and cruises up and down Christmas Tree Lane in Santa Rosa, California, where every homeowner participates in spectacularly decorating their home. The street is blindingly bright with Christmas lights, reindeers are on rooftops, mechanical Santa and Mrs. Clauses are waving from the lawns, Jesus and Mary are in the stables, and there are lots of other displays. While we make this drive, we sing Christmas carols and tell Christmas stories to each other.

About a month before Christmas, when I was around four years old, Mother and I wrote Santa Claus, telling him what a good girl I had been and what I wished for. Mother knew Santa and Mrs. Claus' address because she worked at the post office.

On Christmas Eve, after putting out cookies and milk for Santa and plenty of carrots for his reindeer, I reluctantly left with my family to view Christmas Tree Lane. This was before I fully understood how special it was going to be, so I was impatient to return home. I really had my heart set on meeting Santa. I was even wearing my pretty pink and green dress, just for him.

When we returned home, I found our stockings already stuffed and presents spilling out from under the tree. You would think I would have been excited and satisfied, but I started to cry. Mother took my hand and led me to a chalkboard Santa had left. To my surprise, he had written a special note, just for me.

"Angela, I'm sorry I missed you and I hope you enjoyed Christmas Tree Lane. There are a lot of other girls' and boys' homes around the world I need to deliver presents to now. Thank you for the cookies and milk and carrots."

There were crumbs left on the plate, the napkin was crumpled, and the carrots were gone. I was satisfied.

— *Angela*

Fourteen

A FISH STORY

The humor of living on the edge of the prairie, some twenty-five miles west of State Street, was that the angle of the cul-de-sac that faced our house across Thornwood Drive suggested a sled run. Never mind that the elevation was probably 3APL (three feet Above Prairie Level). If we had a white December, we greeted Christmas by pretending to blaze down fifty yards of snow-crusted blacktop as if it sloped like the Matterhorn.

I was ten, and undecided on the Santa issue. In any case, I expected the holidays to be overshadowed, or perhaps overwhelmed, or even totally obliterated, by my sister's wedding.

Yet, the tree went up as always on December 19, my brother's birthday. The collection of packages underneath looked sparse compared with other years; not surprising, given the wedding expenses my parents discussed when they thought my ears were otherwise absorbed. To be frank, I was expecting a mediocre haul. And when it was announced that to honor my brother-in-law-to-be's family tradition, we would open presents Christmas Eve, there went Santa.

Mother set a beautiful table for dinner. And I am certain there was ham, and Cold Duck or Sparkling Burgundy, wines that in the Midwest of that era symbolized our quite healthy share of national prosperity. I always had some in a fragile glass that refracted the candlelight in a rosy palette of colors.

During the meal, Father made several unexplained pilgrimages to the rec-room of our vintage-1958, three floor, split level. It was this style home that was about to transform charming suburbs like ours into characterless cities; but for the moment, we were the envy of all.

After *inglemot*, our traditional Swedish "angel food" of crushed butter cookies, whipped cream, and lingonberries, the adults carried coffee into the living room, and I distributed gifts. I don't recall what others received (my parents probably exchanged paid wedding bills), but as a ten-year-old, I can be forgiven for hoping to unwrap something fun. I remember some books and disappointment.

When the platter of cookies was hauled into the living room, my father asked me to go downstairs and fetch a pillow. I imagine the family then stopped talking so as to hear me exclaim over the fifty-gallon aquarium he had erected, filled, and stocked with exotic tropical fish during his absences from the dinner table. It never had occurred to me to want an aquarium, but I was thrilled. The wedding hadn't chased me out of the Christmas picture after all.

Everyone came downstairs to share my delight. There were multicolored Siamese fighting fish with tails that swooped like scimitars; pucker-lipped angelfish, so thin they nearly vanished when they turned sideways; ordinary guppies that were *de rigueur* in a Midwestern fish tank at that time; as well as other bright species I no longer recall, along with plants and gravel at the bottom. There was even a little castle and a bubble apparatus that aerated the water.

I kept running downstairs all evening to enjoy my new pets, and it wasn't until years later that I read that a "floater" is what homicide detectives call a corpse found in a river or lake. About an hour later, an upside-down guppy rose to the surface of the aquarium and slowly moved along the glass, a "floater," propelled by the bubbler. My father retrieved it with a small net and gave it an Illinois-style burial at sea by flushing it down the toilet. Fifteen minutes later, another fish died. Then another, and by 10:00 P.M., they had all taken the plunge.

My father promised to restock the tank the day after Christmas. It was at the pet shop we learned that the water needs to "rest" for twenty-four hours before it can support aquatic life. The second school of fish lived and provided endless entertainment—and my sister's wedding was the event of the year.

— *David*

Fifteen

A JEWISH CHRISTMAS

As a Jewish kid, come Christmas when I was about nine, I was allowed to lobby for one particular gift I wanted Mr. and Mrs. Santa Claus-Gribben to deliver so that I might be truly thankful instead of stony-faced polite. There was a cowboy outfit I saw in a box at the toy store. Actually, all I saw was the picture on the outside of the box, but that quickly became my Christmas fantasy.

Guess what? I got that box on Christmas morn; and when I opened it, the pile of beige cloth did in no way resemble the crisp black hat, red shirt, and black vest depicted on the box. And the gun wasn't even close, either. I had been gypped! I was miserable. My heart was broken.

My mom called her friend, the store owner, and asked for an explanation, which turned out to be: "What's inside doesn't have to fit the picture on the outside."

Isn't that the law of the universe? Forget about gravity and relativity. How many times does the outside fool us? Too many to count? We're talking infinity here. It has humbled me to the point where I now accept all losses as just another example that I've got to appreciate the inside before I can enjoy the outside. That lesson has been my all-time, best Christmas gift.

As for the cowboy outfit, I wore it until it disintegrated.

— *Simon*

LITTLEST ANGEL

At the tender age of nine, I had been selected to be one of the angels in the Christmas pageant at the First Presbyterian Church. It was to be held on stage in the large basement of the church.

To say I looked angelic in my white robe and wings would be a vast understatement. I was extremely proud, and very excited.

The pageant, which was the telling of *The Christmas Story*, was going smoothly. I was on stage with the other angels foretelling the coming of Jesus to the shepherds, and I happened to glance at the audience. Actually, I looked to where my sister Ann sat with her two best friends, Jo Lane Thorwarth and Nancy Hunter. There was Nancy, hands up to each ear, flapping her fingers, and sticking out her tongue at me.

Without thinking and with lightning reflex action, I mimicked her perfectly, with both hands, fingers, and tongue.

The astonishment of the audience in seeing their littlest angel sticking out her tongue and with her thumbs in her ears, waving her fingers at them, completely silenced the room. Then, after a moment, they all began to laugh.

That is, all except for my mother. I'll never forget that look. *And*, she wasn't laughing.

— *Mary Lee*

THE MAGIC OF CHRISTMAS

The year my children seemed to be the perfect age for Christmas magic was when Lucas had just turned six and Alyssa was two. In first grade and preschool, the knowledge that Santa Claus is real is as much a fact as the color of the sky or the need to finish all the ice cream before the first tiny bit melts.

We always spent Christmas Eve at Grandpa's so that Christmas morning could be at home. This meant that just as the adults felt they had a few moments to enjoy a glass of wine or a cup of coffee, the children who normally would clamor to stay awake, began to tug at the hands of their parents, knowing that the sooner they got to their beds the sooner Santa would visit their house.

When we got home, my son, the six-year-old veteran, flew up the stairs and into his pajamas, fast asleep before the room even got dark. Alyssa was a little more hesitant, but soon followed the lead of her brother. Daddy and I still had Christmas work to do, so we were up slightly longer.

I had hardly gotten into bed and closed my eyes when a little hand began to pull at me. "Mommy," I heard, "you left the lights on downstairs."

"No, I didn't, honey, go back to sleep," I replied. But Alyssa would not relent. Pulling me from my bed, more by will power than force, she led me to the stairs.

We went down together. As we reached the landing where we could see the tree all lit up and surrounded with presents, I felt her hand squeeze mine with a sudden intensity and heard her breath leave in a gasp.

"We gotta go to bed!" she exclaimed, and raced back up the stairs. As I lay back down a few moments later, I felt the magic of Christmas more vividly than I had since I was a child myself. I'll never forget that moment of shock and pure joy.

— *Lisa*

STOCKING STUFFERS

I received my favorite Christmas gift in December of 1951. Under the tree was a box in plain brown paper that had arrived in the mail a few days before. It was from the young man I had been dating in Texas. It was a box of Whitman's chocolates. The box was called an "antique box."

After all the gifts were opened, my mother said, "I think you liked the box of candy best."

"You're right, Mom," I agreed.

I still have that antique box, only now it's filled with letters from that boy in Texas—my husband of fifty-one years.

— *Cissy*

Sometimes I think I have the worst luck of all. My birthday is December 24th, and my family opens our Christmas gifts on Christmas Eve. My gifts always say "for birthday and Christmas." Somehow that just doesn't seem fair. To this day, as a grown man, I still get doubled-up at Christmas.

— *Allan*

This is one of those little known Christmas facts: As the millennium approached, Rudolph signed with a new agent. He then ruffled a few feathers by wanting to renegotiate his contract with Santa Claus. There was a stalemate, and I was thrown into the breach. With a red flashlight in my beak, attached to a battery under my right wing, I hitched up and led the way. That's why in 1999 there was an egg under every Christmas tree!

— *The Famous Chicken*

The most memorable Christmas? I have many: That first cool bicycle Santa Claus somehow managed to squeeze down the chimney. The first Christmas when I bought my parents something I thought they really wanted, with my very own money. The Christmas Eve I told Mom and Dad I was going to ask Julie to marry me. The first Christmas with my wife. The first time I got to be Santa and stayed up until 3:00 in the morning putting together a simple racetrack, that promised "some" assembly required . . . .

— *Leon*

The year was 1941. The big movie was *Sun Valley Serenade* starring Sonja Henie, and I absolutely fell in love with her. On Christmas morning, right under the lights on the tree was my official, ice-skating, Sonja Henie doll. I spent all Christmas Day on a little frozen pond in front of our house, skating with my doll. It was my best Christmas ever.

— *Ann*

Christmas is important. When we married, Lillian agreed to have a Jewish home provided we celebrate Christmas. In 1968, we were in our first home—a small stucco structure with spectacular views set on two acres in the community of Rancho Santa Fe. On that Christmas Eve, we stayed up most of the night decorating the tree and putting together presents for our children.

The sun came up, but it was very cold. We lit a fire. It still burns.

— *Don*

Although I accompanied my Dad to the St. Joseph's Orphan Home for Girls every year to "help Santa," I didn't know at the time that my dad *was* Santa.

I remember one Christmas when each of the little girls at the orphanage got a doll, a doll's bed with pillows and a blanket, and a small trunk full of wonderful clothes for their dolls. Seeing so many little girls together at such a special time made me wish I could be one of them.

— *Marty*

Throughout my childhood, I always received a gift from my aunt who was known as "the richest widow in Central Ohio." One Christmas, I got a pair of dime store white socks that were too large. The next year I got a clip-on necktie that was too small. The worst was two used, rewrapped, small bars of Pullman soap from an overnight trip she had taken on the B&O Railroad. I always figured her Christmas frugality was the basis of her wealth.

— David

When my daughter, Blair, was little, we went to Hawaii for the holidays. She was a great traveler, and always felt safe as long as she had her blanket—her "B" along. Then one Christmas Eve, when we came back to our hotel from dinner, the maids had cleaned the room and "B" was missing.

I took one look at Blair's tear-stained face and proceeded to the basement, where the laundry for five hundred-plus guests was rotating in industrial-sized washing machines. Wide-eyed service people gathered behind picture windows to watch the crazy blond lady crawling through wet and dry laundry dressed in her holiday best.

I finally located the thread-bare, pink and blue blanket and proudly presented it to my child. To this day, Blair still remembers her Santa Claus-Mommy crawling through all that dirty laundry.

— *Judith*

I can't remember anything worthwhile about Christmas. I do, however, remember a couple of holidays while you and I were working together that we would exchange a fifth of bourbon. Then on Christmas Eve, we would drink mine and you would take yours home. If I think of anything else worthwhile, I'll get back to you.

— *Jack*

Eighteen

CHRISTMAS IN CHICAGO

In mid-December 1973, right before my tenth birthday, my mother, brother, and I rode the train to Chicago for the Christmas holidays. My father was already there, filling in as sports anchor at WMAQ-TV. We didn't want him to spend the holidays alone.

We stayed at The Executive House Hotel in downtown Chicago, and there was snow everywhere. I thought this was so cool, considering I lived in Southern California where snow is rare, even in our local mountains.

Dad arranged for a limo to show us the sights, and George, the limo driver, took us wherever we wanted to go. But our most special trip was to a Christmas tree lot where we found the perfect tree, which George then tied to the roof of the limo.

Arriving back at the hotel, the man at the front desk immediately nixed our intention of dragging our tree through the lobby and up to our room. He told us very sternly, "That's a fire hazard."

Mother had a better idea. After again tying the tree onto the limo, George drove us around to the back of the hotel. From there, we sneaked the tree up to our room via the service elevator.

Once in our room, we decorated the tree the old fashioned way— with strings of popcorn and cranberries. We even made a paper garland out of the hotel stationery, and topped the tree off with a large star made from aluminum foil. Our tree was beautiful!

Christmas arrived and Santa brought me the biggest stuffed Raggedy Ann and Andy dolls I had ever seen! I still have them—as I do the memories of our family sharing that special Christmas together in Chicago.

— *Julie*

Nineteen

CHRISTMAS IN NEW YORK

In December 1945, I was in the Army Air Corps at Camp Shanks, just out of New York City, when I found out we were being pulled out of aircraft mechanics school to be sent overseas. We were to be replacements for those who were there at the end of the fighting in World War II.

Camp Shanks was cold with lots of snow that December. We were told that those living close could have Christmas Day off. But since I didn't know anyone in New York City, I was already planning a lonely Christmas.

Then on Christmas Eve, the phone rang for me in headquarters. A friend of my father's, who lived in New York City, invited me to come to their house on Christmas Day. I was to ride the bus into New York and then take the elevated train to where they lived.

They met me at the station and took me to their home. They had not opened their presents, as they had waited. They even had a warm scarf under the tree for me!

After a delicious dinner and a visit by their priest, they took me back to catch the elevated train and bus back to camp. What a nice surprise for a lonely private. It turned out that the warm scarf was the perfect gift, as the next day we shipped out for

Germany, and I spent the following year at Templehof Airdrome in Berlin.

Now, more than fifty-five years later, I still remember their kindness, and try to repay it by sharing our Christmas dinner with those who may find warmth and good cheer in our company.

— *Ira*

Twenty

WEIHNACHTEN IN BERLIN

My most memorable Christmas is being a child in postwar World War II Berlin. We were living in one of the few buildings left standing on our street. Money was tight and food was sparse, but Christmas was special.

The anticipation of being allowed to enter the living room on Christmas Eve after dark was keeping my sister and me jittery. When the door finally opened and we saw the tree—very small, but so beautiful, glowing with real wax candles—it took our breath away.

The presents were very few. A plate called "Bunter Teller" filled with sweets, nuts, and apples. A hand-knitted sweater. A pair of mittens. One toy. But it was so very special to us.

Since then, my Christmases have gotten richer with presents, but not as rich as the warm feeling of getting my first glimpse of that little glowing tree as a child in Berlin.

— *Ingrid*

Twenty-one

CHRISTMAS IN LONDON

As a toddler in London, I recall being awakened in the middle of the night and carried down to the Anderson shelter at the end of the garden, to escape the onslaught of nighttime bombs during World War II. Later, I remember starting kindergarten and having to carry a box with me everywhere I went—not a lunch box, but one that contained my gas mask.

The first Christmas I remember was when I was six and the war was over. Some weeks prior to Christmas, my parents had saved their ration coupons and managed to get together the ingredients for a real English Christmas Pudding, much to the delight of the entire family. It would be cooked and held for several weeks so that everything could meld together in the traditional manner.

In our tiny kitchen, smaller than a walk-in closet, my father, the baker, was stirring up the mix in a big yellow bowl, and I was jumping up and down with excitement. The pudding was ready to go into the pot for steaming.

Then the unimaginable happened. I knocked the bowl off the table onto the tile, where it smashed to smithereens. My father was furious and sent me to my room.

The "tragedy" was not mentioned again, but I was terrified. Not only would we not have Christmas Pudding, but I was sure Santa would pass me by for my sin!

The great day came, and I awoke with trepidation. But I need not have worried. Santa had presented me with my first doll, and what a beauty she was! I was thrilled!

But Christmas lunch had yet to be served, and I was sure that it would be quite constrained due to the lack of the "centre piece." You can imagine my surprise and relief when my mother presented a small but respectable pudding and my brothers cheered. It seems that we had enough ingredients to make yet another after I had ruined the first, and it all turned out happily. My punishment was not knowing until Christmas Day.

This may seem like a small incident of no great consequence and easily forgotten, but when Christmas arrives, it always comes to mind.

— *Anne*

— Twenty-two —

CHRISTMAS IN PANAMA

When I was eleven years old, my family lived in the small Central American country of Panama. My father had been an engineer at the beginning of the construction of the Panama Canal in 1909. In 1941, he was called back to help with the construction of an additional lock to the Canal. Since the project would take several years to complete, my parents determined that staying together as a family would be the only option.

Having grown up in America, it didn't take me long to realize that life in Panama would be different in many ways. One important difference was the weather. While I had been accustomed to four distinct seasons, there was now only one season—hot and humid.

As the months passed and December approached, it was mysterious to me that one could think about Christmas without cold weather and the possibility of snow. Everyone knew that Santa Claus needed snow to travel by reindeer and sleigh from house to house to deliver toys and gifts.

Even though there were no trimmed and decorated Christmas trees, the date on the calendar made us aware that Christmas Day was near, and plans were made to celebrate. Our mothers began to bake Christmas cookies and the traditional fruitcake. Though it didn't feel like Christmas, at least it smelled like Christmas! We practiced singing carols and were given parts to play in *The Christmas Story*.

On December 7, 1941, an event occurred so terrible that all our happy thoughts were interrupted and immediately replaced with fear. Pearl Harbor had been attacked by the Japanese. The American Government was very concerned that the Panama Canal would be a prime target for the Japanese. The Canal was a strategic waterway that could be used to transport military troops and quickly put battleships into the Pacific. They thought the possibility of an attack could be imminent.

Suddenly, life in the Canal zone changed as it became a war zone with military troops coming in by ships and antiaircraft guns rumbling down the streets. Air raid drills were practiced, and the electricity was turned off at dusk and wasn't turned back on until daylight.

The baking our mothers were doing for the holidays became food baked and taken to the U.S.O. Parents thought it would be safer for children if they returned to the United States. It seemed all haste must be made to do what we could to be ready if an attack should come.

As the time grew closer to the 25th of December, the decision was made that the children could stay, and thoughts once again turned to Christmas. Indeed, if ever we should celebrate the birth of Jesus and remember the meaning of His birth, it was certainly now. So, along with keeping in mind the added changes in our daily routine, we returned to singing carols and practicing for the play.

Christmas Eve came and we all gathered in the auditorium, which served as a movie theater on weekdays and as a church on

Sunday. The windows were covered with dark cloth and by candlelight we all sang carols and relived *The Christmas Story*. We put thoughts of the war aside and turned them instead to the birth of Jesus and His promise of Peace on Earth.

Christmas Day came and our prayers were lifted up in thanksgiving that Santa Claus came, and not the Japanese.

— *Joe*

Twenty-three

CHRISTMAS IN THE PERSIAN GULF

Saddam Hussein invaded Kuwait the first week of August 1990, and this marked the beginning of Desert Shield/Storm. A few days later, I found myself on a plane heading for the Persian Gulf.

All I knew about that area was: it was hot, hostile, and unpredictable. I was terrified as to what my duties might entail. I was stationed in tertiary hospitals behind the front lines, where I provided medical support for our injured troops.

When first deployed, we were told that we would be home in a couple of months, most likely before Thanksgiving. Well, Thanksgiving came and went. Next we were told we would be home before Christmas.

As luck would have it, the situation in Kuwait did not improve. We were then told they didn't know when we would get to go home. As you can imagine, our optimism and spirits were knocked down pretty hard.

I remember feeling homesick and angry at the whole deal. Then I looked around, and realized that the rest of my team were in the same predicament. Many were away from home and family for the very first time. It was then I knew that these men were now my family; and, depending on how the fighting in Kuwait and the surrounding area escalated, they may be the last friendly faces I would ever see. So, I decided to make the best of a bad situation.

As Christmas approached, we got together in a room at the Gulf Hotel in Bahrain and shared stories, care packages, and had dinner and drinks at the hotel restaurant and bar. Then a couple of my teammates and I took the festivities a step further. We made a makeshift Christmas tree in the room and decorated it with condoms. It was our way of saluting Saddam Hussein and everything his regime stood for. Needless to say, we had a really bad hangover the next day.

I finally left the Persian Gulf in March 1991. I thank God for getting me home safe, and I'm extremely grateful to all my former teammates for helping make a terrifying Christmas far from home more bearable.

I would also like to thank all of the men and women in the Armed Forces for sacrificing their time with their families and putting themselves in harm's way to defend our freedom.

— *Gary*

Twenty-four

CHRISTMAS IN NEW DELHI

"It's going to be a terrible Christmas." That's what my nine-year-old announced.

"Well it's NOT," I said.

In my mind, I wasn't as positive as I sounded. This was 1965 in New Delhi, and our first Christmas in India. The force of Western culture was yet to be felt on that side of our planet. There was no television and no fast food. Two percent of the population was Christian, and many of those were in south India. Christmas got a nod of recognition in the form of a holiday on the 25th in Delhi, but not much else. India was friendlier with the Soviets than the United States. In fact, they had just finished fighting the American-equipped Pakistanis over Kashmir.

But Christmas was not far off, and it was time to buy a tree. Off I went to the neighborhood nursery. The only variety available was a live cedar tree in a very large bucket of dirt.

It arrived at my front door perched in the middle of a two-wheeled cart (called a tonga) pulled by a half-starved pony and piloted by a ragged, skinny driver and his helper. Together, they wrestled it up the circular stairs to our second floor apartment.

My daughter viewed it as if her worst fears had been realized. I assured her it would be great. "Just wait," I told her, " 'til I go to the wedding street in Chand Ni Chawk Bazaar in Old Delhi".

This is a street of tinsel, glitter, and sparkle, devoted to the necessities of an Indian wedding. All the streets inside the bazaar are small lanes filled with venders carrying a wide array of all things necessary for a wedding, or for a Christmas tree. There are brightly colored turbans, ropes of silver and gold, wonderful bindings and ribbons, beads, sequins, silks, tassels, small shining brass objects, different colored tinsel, real tin foil icicles that will actually tarnish in time, embroidery, and small colorful objects for decorations. There is everything any self-respecting Christmas tree could possibly need to be magnificently and uniquely clad!

On Christmas morning, our tree was gloriously draped with wedding finery, the bucket of dirt was wrapped in a white sheet, and all lit with the little lights used in India to decorate the houses for weddings.

Our gifts were mostly the wonderful crafts of India. Outside, from time to time, different small brass bands appeared and played tunes that had nothing at all to do with Christmas, and often were slightly off key. Nevertheless, they were somehow in the spirit of the season and added to the joy of the day. We all agreed that our first Christmas in India was indeed a great Christmas!

— *Lucy*

— *Twenty-five* —

CHRISTMAS IN AUSTRALIA

There were twenty-four kids under the age of sixteen on our street, and Christmas Eve in Perth was the time for all the families to get together and have a party. When the youngest children got tired, all the older kids would take us to one house and put us to bed to wait for our parents to carry us home when the party was over.

This one particular Christmas Eve, all the kids were assembled in our house. And when the parents finally picked them up, I couldn't get back to sleep, as, like any child, I was waiting for Santa to come.

When I heard some loud bangs and crashes on the front verandah, I looked out through the blinds, thinking I would see Santa dropping off our presents. Instead of Santa, I saw my father and uncle, after a few too many red wines, trying to attach pedals to my sister's new bike. In their inebriated states, they were being very unsuccessful due to the fact that the pedals had a reverse thread and they couldn't work that out. I snuck back to bed thinking I would be in trouble if I got caught.

In the morning when we all awoke, my sister was happy she had a bike, but disappointed she couldn't ride it because the handlebars were on backward and the pedals were taped to the bar in front of the seat.

My father and uncle looked very sheepishly at each other and suggested that Santa was in too much of a hurry to turn the handlebars around and put the pedals on!!!

This is my fondest Christmas story, as it was my first inkling that my father Les and my Uncle John *may* have been assisting Santa a little bit when it came to Christmas present distribution.

— *Darren*

Twenty-six

A "BLENDED-FAMILY"
CHRISTMAS

This was to be our first Christmas as a "blended family." Is not that a hopeful term? Smoothies are blended. Families . . . ha! Anyway, it was to be a new, great tradition, and I prayed that it would be a good one. Nine of us (we parents, plus three by birth, three by marriage, and one by immigration and adoption) would ski together in Lake Tahoe.

December 19th . . . very little snow in Tahoe. But as my mother used to say, "Be careful what you pray for. You just might get it." We had rented a small house just up the hill from town. We would meet in Reno, get a large van, and drive as a group to Lake Tahoe.

December 20th . . . six of us (husband Joe; daughters Angel, Aimee, Anney; son Garrett; and me) got a ride to the airport in San Diego. "Pray for snow," said husband Joe. A ski report gives him his wish. It is snowing in Tahoe.

Daughter Devon is flying into Reno from Los Angeles. Daughter Stormy is coming in from studying in Paris. Son Dino would arrive from Denver.

1:00 P.M. . . . we are at the airport, only to learn that our 2:30 flight is delayed. But there should be perfect powder by tomorrow.

4:00 P.M. . . . 5:00 P.M. . . . 6:00 P.M. . . . still in San Diego. Still snowing in Nevada. There is already four feet of the new stuff. Some of the family has stopped praying.

Four more hours pass. After some negotiating, I convince one of the many pay phone "divas" to let me have a few minutes to contact Devon and Dino, who are waiting in Reno. As we talk, Stormy arrives in Reno from Paris.

11:00 P.M. . . . our flight is canceled. We can leave tomorrow at 4 P.M. NO WE CAN'T!

11:05 P.M. . . . our three in Reno rent a room.

11:10 P.M. . . . there's a flight leaving Las Vegas at 7:00 A.M. for Reno (Las Vegas is only five-and-a-half hours away from San Diego at 65 mph)

11:20 P.M. . . . I declare, "The snow praying is officially OVER!"

11:30 P.M. . . . we rent the only car left at San Diego's Lindberg Field airport—a Chevy Cavalier . . . a comfortable car for four small people.

11:40 P.M. . . . the six of us pile in and head for Las Vegas.

3:00 A.M. . . . we're in Victorville (more than half way now). A radio report says Lake Tahoe has been hit with ten feet of snow so far. We begin praying for an end of the snow. One of us then added, "And even a little melt, maybe."

5:30 A.M. . . . here we are . . . Las Vegas!

7:00 A.M. . . . flight to Reno ON TIME. Still snowing in Lake Tahoe.

Summary to-date and highlights of what is to come:

Three nights in Reno waiting for the roads to open to Tahoe equals three rooms, three nights at $200 per body; add food for nine for three days at hotel prices.

Joe went to the casino to recoup losses. He said he prayed for wisdom at the blackjack table. He got it: "It is wise NOT to sit at the blackjack table." I think you can do the math.

Rented van sits for three days waiting. It's Christmas Eve.

The roads are cleared of the sixteen-plus feet of snow (a new record for one storm)!

Up the mountain, stopping only to put special chains on the wheels (special equals = $$$).

I pray for patience and am given many opportunities.

We are told by the rental office that our house is ready. House, yes . . . road, no.

We park in town and hike up the hill. Here's some more math for you: sixteen feet of snow . . . fourteen feet of house!

Dino swims in to open the door as Garrett creates a high path.

We are all exhausted after getting a small tree up . . . well, not exactly straight up, but it fit the mood.

Anney says, "I'm so tired, I wish we weren't going to Midnight Mass." (Wishes can be like prayers; refer back to "Careful what you wish for.")

We go to the hospital instead. Luckily, Anney doesn't have food poisoning . . . only acute indigestion.

Christmas Day . . . church . . . dinner . . . family laughing together, and we *almost* went skiing. It rained (refer back to praying for snow to melt).

Christmas night . . . the 10:00 P.M. shuttle from Harrah's in Reno to Harrah's, Lake Tahoe has flat tire. Future son-in-law, Chris, aboard. The four-hour wait for Chris at Harrah's teaches Joe a new game: "Let It Ride" (more aptly named, "Leave It Here"). Joe gains more wisdom.

December 26 . . . Joe and daughter Angel go to pick up future son-in law Jamie at Harrah's. He's not there. After many phone disconnects, we learn he's at a Harrah's in some other Nevada City . . . not Lake Tahoe.

While waiting for the new shuttle to arrive, Joe finds a brand new game called Pey Gow. New wisdom: PAY GOUGE!

We did manage to get in two days of some pretty fair skiing. No broken bones, although Joe ran down a few people on the slopes. Fortunately, it was usually family.

Aimee pretty much summed up the trip when she would occasionally lie on the dining room table and proclaim loudly, "AGHHHHHHHHHHHHHHHHHHH!!"

With all the trials and tribulations, however, I must say we became a family that Christmas . . . not *in spite* of it all, but *because* of it all. And I thank God yet today for answering my prayer on our first Christmas as a "blended family."

— *Mary Ann*

— *Twenty-seven* —

CELEBRATE LIFE

My favorite Christmas was the one just past because of how truly it taught me the spirit of Christmas.

It has become a tradition in my family to gather with relatives from my dad's French-Italian side to celebrate Christmas and my grandma's birthday. This year we were gathering for her eighty-sixth birthday, and also in celebration of her triumph over non-Hodgkin's lymphoma. A family portrait was arranged to capture the group that had grown to include grandchildren as well as great-grandchildren.

As a surprise, my dad and his two brothers arranged for a friendly roast of my grandma, to recount memories of her life as a devoted wife, loving mother, and caring grandmother. Thus, a woman dressed as a reindeer arrived shortly after dinner to recount my grandmother's life story and how her patience and acceptance of others has filled our family with love. As the stories were told, one could see the delight and pride in my grandma's eyes as she looked around the room at all the lives she had touched.

I remember the balmy-cool "Southern California" weather, the Italian dishes, my grandma's delicious, lovingly made, holiday pies, and the laughter that filled my parents' home during that party.

Today, our family portrait hangs in my home as a reminder of that special day when the family gathered for a holiday that was fated to be the last time we would all gather together. My grandma recently succumbed to the non-Hodgkin's lymphoma that reared its ugly head again.

She knew it was her time to leave us. Knowingly, each visit to her bedside in the hospital and eventually in her home was spent recounting family memories. She gave us a special gift this past Christmas: a simple reminder of how showing others that they are loved can build a resilient family. While she has left us for a better place, we continue to celebrate her life by carrying on the traditions of family, cooking Italian food, appreciating art and nature, and gathering together to share a meal and good company. For many Christmases to come, we will gather like others as a family to celebrate life and one another.

— *Jeanette*

Twenty-eight

THE MEANING OF CHRISTMAS

It was Christmas Eve, 1970. I was fourteen years of age, and as was our want at this time, we invited Elders of the Church of Jesus Christ of Latter-Day Saints over to our home for a dinner and a spiritual lesson. As ardent members of said church, this is a tradition that we have kept up for quite some time. In fact, one Christmas we had a gentleman read the entire text from "The Other Wise Man."

After we had finished dinner, we went into the front room for our discussion and video presentation. I use that last part loosely, because it was on an overhead projector, just to give you an idea as to how long ago this was. It was a brand-new projector and it kept giving off a smell that was noticeable—at least, that is what we thought it was.

But the third time someone said they smelled something, my mother opened the door back to the dining room. It was then we discovered that flames were licking the walls at a rapid rate, and we had a full-blown fire on our hands.

In retrospect, we were quite fortunate. If my mother had waited just a minute later, the fire would have lept out at her and she could have been severely burned. We had eaten by candle-light and evidently none of us thought to blow the candles out as we went into the front room.

While that was certainly unfortunate, what turned out to be our really good fortune was the fact that the fire department was only a half-mile away. To their credit—remember, this is Christmas Eve—they hustled over in less than ten minutes and did an excellent job of dousing the flames, preserving about half of the house.

On the downside, they did not get there in time to save my eight-year cover collection of *Sports Illustrated*, reaching all the way back to Valery Brumel's high jump world record.

With our lives now irrevocably changed, we were jarred back into reality as to what were we going to do? What happened next was something that could have been written as a true "The Meaning of Christmas" story. One by one, neighbors, some that we did not even know, came by to offer their homes to us, as well as meals, clothes, money, transportation—whatever was needed.

In retrospect, I would like to believe that they did this because we had the local paper route and they liked us. But truth be known, it was simply a matter of a Christlike charity that fills the soul when something untoward happens to another. "Inasmuch as ye have done it unto the least of these, my brethren, ye have done it unto me."

After the many offers for help, my father kindly asked for some privacy, and we went into the backyard amidst the pungent aroma of smoke (that would not leave the house until I did for college). He gathered us together, looked us all in the eye, and simply said, "We're all right."

I remember the swelling of my being as it finally hit me that material things were *not* that big a deal and that, despite the miraculous discovery that presents were strewn around the house uncharred, I genuinely did not care. We had come together as a family and responded the way we should have, thanks to a vigilant father and a supportive mother who had taught us there was more to life than accumulating *things*.

I learned that night that the greatest elixir of all is HOPE, and that people, despite their myriad flaws and perpetual insensitiveness to the human condition, can also rise to the occasion and reveal a charity unknown in common hours. This was a Yuletide that changed my life for the better in a way that is unquantifiable. I owe my parents, Ned and June Christensen, an unpayable debt that I can hopefully pass on to my progeny as they celebrate their own Noels . . . and hardships.

— *Todd*

Twenty-nine

WHITE GOLD

About twenty years ago, I moved from the Philippines to the mountains of Idaho with my then-husband and three-year-old son and five-year-old daughter. None of us had ever seen or even heard of snow before.

The first time it got cold and snowed, I looked out the window and saw "white" falling from the sky. I didn't know what it was, and I was very afraid. When I gathered my children to see this strange spectacle, my son said he thought it was "white gold from God."

We had never been in cold weather before and didn't know anything about winter clothes. So when our neighbors saw us outside looking at the snow without coats or sweaters, they came out and explained what snow was.

I would walk my children to school some three miles each day because I could not drive. The first time I got the children to school in the cold, their little hands and mine were all blue. The teacher gave me her gloves and explained that I needed to get winter clothes for everyone.

We didn't know how Christmas was done here in the United States, but we soon found out. At Christmas, gifts for all of us arrived from the townspeople. Inside the colorful wrappings were warm clothes for the entire family.

I didn't speak very much English at that time, but I was so very grateful to them for their generosity. Even now, I weep when I think of how much those gifts meant to our family, and for the first time, we understood the spirit of Christmas.

— *Sally*

— *Thirty* —

SNOW ANGELS

Christmas of 2000 was my favorite because I had found Steve, the love of my life and my future husband. We had gone together to his sister's house in Denver, Colorado, for the holidays.

I grew up in Ventura, California, the baby of nine kids, as a beach goin', boogie boardin', inner tubing, sandcastle building, little string bean of a red-head kid. I had seen the snow, and even played in it in the mountains, but I had never seen it fall.

So, celebrating Christmas in Denver, Steve and I had some big expectations of winter. Crossing our fingers, we wished on all the stars we saw in the sky on that clear, Christmas Eve, and listening to carols and an occasional weather report of "possible snow on Christmas," we sent good thoughts to Santa . . . "Bring Rose snow!"

Christmas morning, I got up, turned on the tree, and twinkling lights began to fill the room with joy. Then, hearing a soft tic-tic-tic noise against the windowpane, I looked out. A light, gentle, snow was covering all of Denver—the rooftops, the trees, the grass—with a beautiful white blanket of snowflakes.

Our wish came true!!! There is a Santa!!! I think I woke up the entire household with my laughter and shouts of joy.

Still in my clumsy, winter PJs, I ran out the front door, threw myself on the quarter-inch of snowfall, and immediately began to make the sweetest snow angels you have ever seen. I was completely filled with happiness and joy.

Sticking out my tongue, I could feel the cold, tingling of the snowflakes falling into my mouth. Opening up my hand to the sky, I felt for the first time, tiny snowflakes gently resting in my palm, melting immediately before I could muster up my best version of a snowball.

Then I saw Steve, smiling with laughter as he looked down at my disheveled, melted angel. He dropped down to join me in the snow, swinging his arms and legs. Suddenly, we had two angels. Then we scooted side by side, each swinging one arm and one leg, creating the perfect connected angel, together as one.

At that moment, I realized how simple Christmas and life really is. And I didn't need anything else in that moment. Nothing in the whole world could have made me happier.

— *Rose*

Thirty-one

MY FUTURE REVEALED

Mine is a strange and yet wonderful memory of Christmas Eve. I was a senior in high school and going steady, but still very unsure what my future might hold.

On this particular Christmas Eve, we double-dated for midnight Mass but arrived a little late. Consequently, the four of us had to stand against the back wall, just to the right of where we entered the church. It was quite crowded and very warm, and all of a sudden I fainted. I had never fainted before and have never fainted since.

When I came to, I was outside the church in the cold of a Southern Christmas Eve. I was being held in the arms of my steady, and I could feel snowflakes gently falling on my face.

I knew in that moment that my future had been decided. I wanted to spend the rest of my life in those strong arms. And I have.

We've been married now for twenty-five years, and have three wonderful girls. And I continue to celebrate every Christmas Eve in his arms.

— Name withheld by request

Thirty-two

CHRISTMAS EXTRAVAGANZA

Several years ago, I was asked by our church to create a "Christmas Musical Extravaganza," and I cheerfully accepted.

After months of writing, casting, rehearsing, and coordinating with a production team and a cast of over fifty including a camel, a donkey, and some sheep, preparation was completed. The Chancel Choir and Orchestra would supply the music. The advertising agency that had assisted with the script would also supply the sound effects and voices of God and the angels.

As the lights dim on opening night, the orchestra begins to play, and the silence is broken by the voice of God, "In the beginning . . . ." The production was proceeding beautifully. The angel Gabriel announces the birth of Christ. Mary and Joseph begin coming down the aisle . . . .

Then it happens. The donkey on which Mary is riding becomes stubborn and starts bucking. Mary manages to safely get off, and she then walks with Joseph and the donkey to the manger scene. The choir begins to sing of the birth of Jesus, and I start to breath again.

The shepherds and their sheep surround the Holy Family at the manger. Our son, Chris, the sandal-wearing, lead shepherd, is caught off guard by the necessity of the sheep to relieve themselves all over his feet.

At about this time, the camel coming down the aisle with the procession of Wise Men begins to spit on the audience. The cast is dutifully trying to ignore these problems, but my good friend, who happens to be helping us with the sound system, is lying on the floor of the choir loft in controlled stitches of laughter.

Everything that could go wrong did. But when the angels announced the birth of Christ and the choir and orchestra began the *Magnificat*, all problems were forgotten. The "Extravaganza" came to a glorious end, with the congregation aglow in the light of hundreds of candles. The Christmas spirit was alive and well all around us.

— *Bob*

Thirty-three

TWELVE DAYS OF CHRISTMAS

I've never been a particularly patient person, and it was very difficult as a youngster to see all the gaily wrapped and beribboned presents pile ever higher under the Christmas tree and have to wait *all* the way to Christmas Eve to find out what was in them.

Although my younger brother and I were sternly admonished not to touch, this did not stop us from much acrobatic craning of necks and contortions of bodies to learn which ones were ours, and, if we were really lucky, which ones did not feel like clothing.

The year we reached the age where we would not be leaving a plateful of cookies for Santa on Christmas Eve, the piles of gifts accumulating under our tree took on new significance. *Now* they included the gifts Santa used to bring! And parental surveillance tightened accordingly.

My tactics needed to change. I soon discovered that if I were to get sick just before church the Sunday preceding Christmas Eve, I could count on at least two hours of uninterrupted time to carefully open and then carefully rewrap all my gifts.

Okay, I can hear you gasp. I'm not saying it was right. But I will tell you it was right for me, and still is to this very "sixty-something" day.

It's my own private, traditional Christmas that starts whenever I receive and immediately open my very first gift. That opening expands to include the giving and receiving of all my loved ones' and friends' gifts throughout the Christmas season. That way, my Christmas truly does last the twelve days of Christmas . . . and sometimes more.

One day is just not enough!

— *Caran*

Thirty-four

A SPECIAL PRESENT

A long time ago in a place far away—a place I call Minnesota—I enjoyed many a wonderful wintery Christmas. This was in part because of a special present that was under the tree every year.

This wonderful gift came repacked in different sizes . . . always in different Christmas paper . . . but always with the same thing inside. And always from the same special uncle.

Uncle Scotty was full of tricks and great stories—the kind of stories I still want to believe. Sometimes he would tell us about chasing Pancho Villa back into Mexico or about saving kids from certain disaster—kids who had disobeyed their parents and snuck into the old widow woman's yard late at night.

Sometimes he told us about fishing with chewing tobacco, which makes perfect sense. You throw the tobacco in the water. The fish chew it. Then when they come up to spit, you grab 'em. It's true!

The different size box and different gift wrapping was part of his game. And, of course, it became a Christmas tradition.

The present . . . a box of chocolate-covered cherries . . . the syrupiest, sugariest, *sweeeeetest* things ever. I don't remember ever liking them, but no one knows that . . . well, not until now. I would bring them to school to share (translation: get rid of 'em). But it was this tradition, which had nothing to do with the present, and it had everything to do with who it was from.

Christmas was not Christmas until I found that mysterious box. This went on through high school and college and even after I left this frozen land of the loon (Minnesota's state bird . . . the loon. And all this time you thought it was the mosquito!).

No matter where I was with my new family, a package would arrive at Christmastime . . . always a different size, always uniquely wrapped. I would say to my kids, "I wonder what's in here?" And the kids would say, "We know, we know. Let's open it . . . but first, Daddy, you have to tell us a Christmas story about kids who disobey or your Christmas with Pancho what's-his-name, you know . . ." Well, I'd do that. We'd open the box . . . we'd all act surprised. The kids would taste one, set it on a plate. I'd take the rest to work . . . to share! Then one year the package didn't come. Uncle Scotty had died that fall.

Several years later a small box arrived in late December at our home in San Diego. I put it under the tree and forgot about it. On Christmas Eve, we were all sitting around the tree opening presents. One of our daughters brought the package to me. "Here's one you didn't open, Dad." When I saw the "different wrapping," I got that little lump in my throat. Sure enough, there they were . . . chocolate-covered cherries . . . with a note that read, "Remember these, Joe?" The note was from Uncle Scotty's sister, my mom. Smiles with tears . . . a fitting combination for that day.

We have several grandchildren now. The oldest was just old enough last Christmas to get her first little mysterious package of . . . (sugar free, low fat) chocolate covered cherries. I wonder if she'll take them to school to share again this year?

— *Joe*

Thirty-five

"CAT BALLOU"

I once spent Christmas Eve in a first floor bungalow of the Hilton Hotel in San Diego. I was living in Dallas at the time, and ABC-TV had assigned me to work the sideline of the American Football League Championship Game between the Chargers and the Boston Patriots the day after Christmas.

This was the year Lee Marvin was nominated for an Oscar for his performance in *Cat Ballou*. This was also the season he adopted the San Diego Chargers, and the Chargers adopted him. Lee had been to all their home games and, naturally, was expected for the Championship game.

That sets the scene:

On Christmas morning, I call room service to order breakfast. "A cheddar cheese omelet, hash browns, toast, and coffee. Bungalow 105. My name is Jones."

"No, it's not."

"What do you mean, 'no, it's not'?"

"Your name's not Jones."

"Then what is it?"

"It's Lee Marvin."

Now, I have no idea why I made the next statement.

"Yes, it is, but I would like to keep it quiet."

"Oh, you can trust me, Mr. Marvin, uh, Mr. Jones. Your breakfast will be there in just a few minutes."

Now the quandary:

Naturally, this young lady will tell everyone in the kitchen, including the young man who will bring the breakfast tray to the room. When I open the door, he will immediately know that I'm not Lee Marvin.

The solution:

I opened the door a crack and clicked the lock so it would stay slightly open. Then I got a ball point pen and went into the bathroom, put the toilet seat down, sat, and waited.

When I heard the knock at the door, I called out in a muffled voice, "I'm in the bathroom. Come on in and put it on the table."

As soon as I heard him moving back across the room, I muffled, "Slide the check under the bathroom door so I can sign it."

He did. The total was $9.70, and I thought, *What the hell, I'm Lee Marvin.* That's the way I signed the check, and I gave the bellman a $20 tip. (Lee would have wanted me to.)

— Charlie

— *Thirty-six* —

CHRISTMAS EVE

During the 1960s, I was a young flight attendant for United Airlines, and was privileged to be a part of the crew that flew our fighting men in and out of Vietnam. The flight I remember most involved the last leg, which was from Honolulu to Travis Air Force Base near San Francisco.

It was Christmas Eve and due to some mechanical glitches, we weren't due to arrive until about midnight.

This was one of those tough flights. These men had been fighting the Viet Cong early that morning, and then had rush orders to clear out in a hurry. Grab what you can and head for the airstrip at Bien Hoa.

They were tired, grubby, and had been sitting on the plane for eighteen hours. Some were even nursing minor injuries. I suspect others had worse wounds that they didn't want to call attention to once they heard they were headed back to "the world," which is what they called anyplace outside of Vietnam.

When fighting in a Vietnam jungle, there's a tendency to forget what day it is. It just doesn't matter. What matters is that it's today. And that you are alive.

So just as a reminder, we decorated the cabin the best we could with red and green ornaments, lots of silver icicles, and, of course, mistletoe. To give you an idea of how beat these men were, not one of our quite attractive and shapely stewardesses was asked for a kiss under the mistletoe!

When the captain finally came on the P.A. and announced an anticipated arrival in the U.S.A. in forty-five minutes, there was an immediate shift. Within moments, there was a mad rush for the "blue rooms." (That's what we called our restrooms.) Grubby fatigues suddenly looked crisp and new. Boots were dusted and shined.

Then one young Marine stepped out of the blue room in the back of the plane and began to quietly sing, "I'll be Home for Christmas." Almost immediately the whole plane joined in. Instead of sitting down, he went up and down the aisle leading us in one carol after another: "Silent Night," "O Come All Ye Faithful," "Joy to the World." Oh, but he had a beautiful voice!

By the time the seat belt sign came on, we were into a hilarious rendition of "The Twelve Days of Christmas," complete with sound effects of "six geese a-laying," "eight maids a-milking," "twelve drummers drumming" and, of course, that old partridge in a pear tree.

As they deplaned down the stairs, every man wished us a warm "Merry Christmas" before stepping back into "the world." At that moment, the clouds parted and "the world" was drenched at that midnight hour in the light of a beautiful full moon.

As I stood in the doorway of that plane and watched them cross the tarmac, all I could think was, "Merry Christmas to all, and to all a good night."

— *Pat Hart*

Merry Christmas